THE SONGS OF ARTURO TOSCANINI

Original Compositions for High Voice & Piano

Contents

SUBITO MUSIC

WWW.SUBITOMUSIC.COM

*The Publisher is grateful to Walfredo Toscanini, Elaine Toscanini, Harvey Sachs
and to Allan Steckler (for the Toscanini Estate) for their help in realizing this edition.*

*A special thank you
to Roger Flury and David Vine
whose dedication and expertise helped make this edition possible.*

TOSCANINI AS COMPOSER

For more than half a century Arturo Toscanini dominated the musical world. He was generally considered to be the greatest conductor of his generation — some might say of any generation — and he played a major role in establishing the popular image of the dictatorial, authoritarian *maestro*. It is an image that remains potent to this day.

Toscanini began his formal music education in 1876, when he was enrolled as a day student at the *Reale Scuola di Musica* in Parma. He was just nine years of age. Within two years, he was awarded a resident scholarship, and by 1884 had become an assistant teacher of harmony. The following year he graduated with maximum marks and honors in violoncello and composition, and won the prize for outstanding student in his year.

The Royal School of Music (now the *Conservatorio di Musica "Arrigo Boito"*) was a bleak institution by today's standards, with long hours of work and strict codes of conduct for students. Fortunately, young Toscanini flourished in this environment, relishing the intensity of musical study — an intensity that was to remain with him for life. Although by no means a model student, he earned the respect of staff and students, as much for his obvious musical ability as for his sharp wit. Under the respected eye of Director Giusto Dacci — himself a prolific composer with over 450 works to his name — Toscanini followed a standard course of study that included theory, keyboard harmony, piano, choral singing, and also some non-music subjects. He was allotted the violoncello as his principal instrument, and his curriculum later expanded to include advanced harmony and composition with Dacci.

Significantly for Toscanini, selected students were permitted to play in the orchestra of Parma's Teatro Regio, and here the young 'cellist was exposed to the operatic scores of Verdi, Donizetti, Meyerbeer, Bizet, Ponchielli, Gounod, Gomes, Pacini, and Wagner — composers whose works formed the core repertoire of the day.

In 1884, a year before his graduation, Toscanini's name appeared on a School of Music concert program in the triple role of 'cellist, composer and conductor. The concert, held in the foyer of the Teatro Regio, offered two of his orchestral works — an *Andante* in E flat and a *Scherzo* in G minor. This was the same year that Wagner's *Lohengrin* was staged in Parma, and its influence can be heard in the clarinet theme and the ethereal divisi string chords in the opening bars of Toscanini's *Andante*. Indeed the influences of Wagner, Verdi, Beethoven and particularly Mendelssohn can be heard in each of his orchestral compositions. This might suggest that Toscanini's music was completely derivative, but we should remember that these are examination pieces, written to satisfy Giusto Dacci. Toscanini knew how to play the game, and wisely gave a nod in the direction of Mendelssohn — the composer whom Dacci held in particularly high esteem — by imbuing the *Scherzo* with something of the spirit of *A Midsummer Night's Dream* without, however, being quite able to match the lightness of touch.

There are two more important orchestral compositions dating from this period — a substantial *Overture* in G major and a fine work for *divisi* violins and 'cellos, *Preghiera alla Vergine*. In addition, there is a curious piece — probably a technical exercise — scored for 4 horns and unison violins, and a substantial four-part *Fuga reale*.

What distinguishes Toscanini's orchestral compositions is not their technical proficiency or orchestration (they pale in comparison to Puccini's youthful pieces), but their anticipation of the passionate, heart-on-sleeve gestures of the *giovane scuola* that were to erupt six years later with the premiere of Mascagni's *Cavalleria rusticana* in 1890. Toscanini's *Preghiera* foreshadows something of the same mood of Mascagni's famous *Intermezzo* and each of the full orchestral pieces contains at its center a soaring theme, given to unison strings accompanied by harp arpeggios, that anticipates the scores of Puccini, Cilea, Mascagni and Giordano.

Within a year of graduating, Toscanini was on a ship bound for South America as principal 'cellist and assistant chorus-master of a touring opera company. On the night of 30 June 1886, he stepped out of the orchestra in Buenos Aires to replace the conductor in a performance of *Aida*. The rest is history.

Toscanini had begun composing in earnest around 1882, at the age of fifteen. By the time he was twenty-one he had produced at least thirty works. Of the chamber compositions, his last is perhaps the most interesting. The title, *Meditazione — Tristezza grave in cor mi piange* (Meditation — My heart weeps with great sadness) is taken from a line in Gabriele d'Annunzio's series of poems, *Malinconia*. Composer Paolo Tosti set *Malinconia* as a cycle of 5 songs, but Toscanini used just one line of text as his inspiration for a composition for violin and piano. That score now appears to be lost, but a version (dated 1888) does exist, scored for solo violin and string quartet. In this unsettling, intense piece, with its persistent syncopated viola heartbeat, one can sense a moment of rare unhappiness in the young Toscanini's life, perhaps an affair of the heart or the loss of a loved one.

1888 was also the year that Toscanini traveled to Bologna to attend a performance of Wagner's *Tristan und Isolde*. The experience was life changing, and he resolved to become a conductor — a comparatively undervalued profession in the Italian opera houses where he would need to seek employment.

Although Toscanini abandoned composition for the remainder of his life, and even tried to prevent widespread distribution and performances of his scores, it should not be assumed that his youthful efforts were unsuccessful. Several pieces were published, most notably a charming, unpredictable *Berceuse* for piano (Giudici & Strada, 1885) and, shortly after his introduction to the publisher Giovannina Lucca in 1886, two songs — *Autunno* (Felice Carlo Cavallotti) and *Nevrosi* (Rocco E. Pagliara).

Four songs were published by Giudici & Strada in 1888 — *Canto di Mignon* (Antonio Ghislanzoni), *Desolazione!* (Enrico Panzacchi), *Son gelosa!!* (Rocco E. Pagliara) and *V'amo* (Heinrich Heine, in an Italian translation). All of these published songs, as well as a further fourteen titles extant only in manuscript copies[1], were probably composed towards the latter end of his student years, between 1882-1885.

The evidence for this assumption lies in the fact that a folio of eight songs, *Otto romanze*, (sold in 2009 by a New York antiquarian dealer to an Italian buyer), is dedicated "Al Distinto Artista di Canto, Antonio Superchi – Omaggio dell' Autore"[2]. Dated "Parma, 18 July 1885", this folio of songs appears to be part of Toscanini's graduation exercise. The Director of the music school, Giusto Dacci, has signed the bottom right hand corner, acknowledging that he has examined the manuscript. The titles in this folio album are (in order) *Sono sola! (per soprano)*, *Son gelosa!! (per mezzo)*, *Fior di siepe (per soprano)*, *Il pescatore (per soprano)*, *Il sorriso e l'anima di Margherita (per tenore)*, *Spes ultima dea (soprano)*, *I baci (per tenore)*, and *Desolazione (per soprano)*. Therefore it seems reasonable to assume that these songs were composed during his last years as a student. *Desolazione!* also exists in a version for voice and orchestra, which we know formed part of his graduation exercise.

At least one song was publicly performed during Toscanini's early career as a conductor. *Son gelosa!!* was presented, and perhaps premiered, by soprano Lola Peydro at her benefit evening during a performance of Ponchielli's *La gioconda* in 1887 at Casale Monferrato. The song reappeared again on 14 April 1889 when it was performed by Adele Borghi at her *serata d'onore* in the Teatro Vittorio Emanuele, Turin. By this time it had been published, with Borghi's name on the cover as dedicatee. In fact, many of his songs bear dedications that suggest they were written for specific performers or friends.

All the songs are characterized by a natural talent for word setting, even if Toscanini's choice of poets is rarely from the top shelf and there is a gloomy preoccupation with lost or unhappy love. Melodically they carry forward the traditions of the *canzoni da camera* of Bellini, Donizetti and Verdi with an occasional nod to Schubert in *Il pescatore* and *V'amo*. At the same time, they anticipate the more liberated art songs of Mascagni, Leoncavallo, Puccini, Zandonai and Respighi. Most significant is the fact that Toscanini rises above the cloying sentimentality that the texts might have inspired from a lesser musician.

Having made the decision to pursue a conducting career, we might wonder why Toscanini felt the need to suppress further performances of his compositions. The scores certainly contain errors that a mature Toscanini would not have countenanced. Some bars are barely sketched in, or left incomplete. He shows a cavalier approach to accidentals, phrasings and poetry, and occasionally he can be seen struggling with difficult harmonic progressions that refuse to fall easily into place; his intentions are clear, but his technical skills are not always able to keep pace with his imagination.

---

[1] The titles are: *Ad una donna* (Giuseppe Giusti), *I baci* and *Presentimenti* (Antonio Ghislanzoni), *Donna vorrei morir, Fior di siepe, Forse una volta, Pagina d'album, Quando cadran le foglie* and *Spes ultima dea* (Lorenzo Stecchetti, pseudonym of Olindo Guerrini), *Per album - Pensiero melodico* (Luigi Arnaldo Vassallo), *Il pescatore* (Anon.), *Primo bacio* (Luigi Morandi), *Sono sola!* (Cesare Cantù), *Il sorriso e l'anima di Margherita* (A. Rossi). Three further songs, *Sogno infantile, Prima perdita,* and *Vicino all'amante*, are mentioned by some biographers, but the location of these manuscripts is unknown.

[2] The Parma-born baritone Antonio Superchi (1816-1898) is remembered now as the creator of the role of Don Carlos in Verdi's *Ernani*, but after his retirement from the stage, he continued to play an influential role in Parma's musical life. It was, therefore, a most diplomatic dedication.

Even the published scores contain mistakes, although it would be unfair to lay all the blame on the composer. He would have had little opportunity to proof read them prior to publication, either because of his peripatetic conducting life or because this task was simply handed to someone whom the publisher considered more experienced.

There has been a distinguished tradition of conductor-composers, from Toscanini's near contemporaries such as Bruno Walter, Victor de Sabata, Felix Weingartner, Otto Klemperer, Albert Coates, Hamilton Harty and Wilhelm Furtwängler to more recent maestros such as Leonard Bernstein, André Previn, Pierre Boulez and Giuseppe Sinopoli. For these men, the need to compose was partly a manifestation of the need to create something new and permanent as opposed to the more ephemeral occupation of interpreting the works of others.

Toscanini, however, felt no such need. He gave himself totally to conducting. Perhaps, the self-imposed suppression of his compositions was also intended to deflect criticism. He was only too aware of his shortcomings in this field, and did not need these pieces of juvenilia held up to public scrutiny, at least not while he was still active.

But we know that Toscanini retained an affection for these youthful works. In a biography of the composer, Harvey Sachs relates how the elderly maestro was challenged to recall some of these long forgotten songs[3]. Proud of his photographic memory, even in old age, Toscanini wrote out nine songs and, in one instance, even attempted to provide a singable English translation. More extraordinary, however, is that errors in the earlier copies, both manuscript and published, were miraculously corrected.

Fortunately for researchers, manuscripts of Toscanini's original compositions are comparatively easy to locate. Many are held at the New York Public Library for the Performing Arts, although only some instrumental works will be found in the magnificent Toscanini Legacy collection donated by the composer's family in 1987. Toscanini was a great friend of the American soprano Rose Bampton and her Canadian husband, conductor Wilfred Pelletier. At some point, Toscanini gifted the songs to Bampton, and it is among her papers at the same institution that these manuscripts are located. Other scores are held at the *Biblioteca Palatina – Sezione musicale* in Parma and at the *Conservatorio di Musica "Giuseppe Verdi"* in Milan. The remainder are presumably in private collections or lost.

In 2007, an antiquarian dealer's catalog unwittingly shed some light on Toscanini's attitude to his compositions. Among the items offered for sale was a sheet of notepaper containing musical autographs of nine leading Italian musicians, collected in Rome between 1930 and 1934. Not surprisingly, all the composers — Pietro Mascagni, Ottorino Respighi, Umberto Giordano, Emmanno Wolf-Ferrari, Vincenzo Tommasini, Francesco Malipiero and Leone Sinigaglia — quoted from their own works. Raffaele Casimiro Casimiri, a composer and musicologist, offered some bars of Palestrina, whose collected works he was editing at the time. Toscanini might have been expected to quote a few bars of Beethoven or Verdi, but instead he offered the opening bars of his song *Canto di Mignon*. This may seem an insignificant gesture, but it does suggest that he was proud enough of his achievement, in this song at least, to unashamedly place it in such distinguished company.

Can we conclude that Toscanini was right — apart from that one moment of immodesty — to keep his youthful compositions a secret? At the time, it may have seemed the right thing to do; to protect an image and suppress negative criticism that could quite easily have diminished his musical authority. Now, more than 120 years after he turned his back on composition, we can examine the scores to reveal a fledgling composer in possession of an emerging individuality, albeit comfortably embedded in the musical vocabulary of the time.

But it is a well known fact that Toscanini could never have found artistic satisfaction in any musical pursuit that was not at the highest level. The music of Wagner — and the score of *Tristan und Isolde* in particular — convinced Toscanini, beyond a shadow of a doubt, that his own musical destiny lay not with the pen, but with the baton.

Roger Flury
Wellington, New Zealand 2009

---

[3] Harvey Sachs. *Toscanini*. London: Wiedenfeld & Nicolson, 1978, p. 29.

Autunno

Pensiero mesto

Felice Carlo Cavallotti

Arturo Toscanini

Da - gli al-be - ri le fo - glie van - no vi - a, Ed il me-sto a-mor

mio co - sì sen va; Sor - ri - de del cre - a - to al - l'a - go -

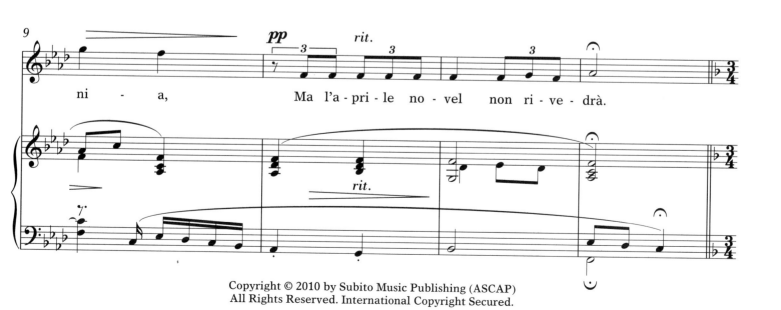

ni - a, Ma l'a - pri - le no - vel non ri - ve - drà.

Po - ve-ro a - mor_____ de' verd' an - ni mie - i Il tor - bi - do de -

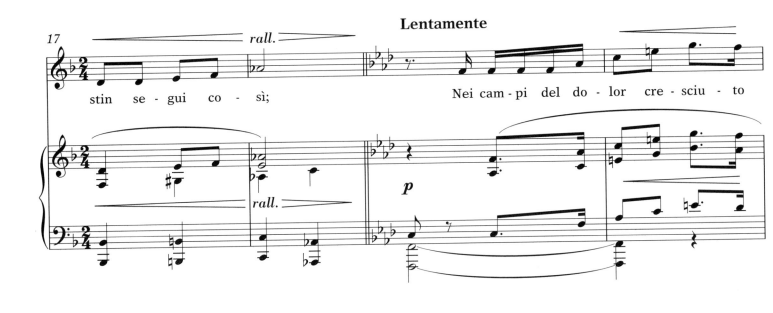

stin se - gui co - sì; Nei cam - pi del do - lor cre - sciu - to

se - i, Or com-pi nel do - lor_____ l'ul - ti - mo dì.

I baci

Romanza

Alfio Belluso

Arturo Toscanini

15

rall.

A noi d'in-tor-no o lez - za-no Ser-ti di gem - me e fior.
Bac-cia-mi o ca-ra e la - scia-mi Di vo-lut-tà mo - rir.

pp rall.

Maggiore

sotto voce

19

cresc.

Po-sa il tuo lab - bro ro - se-o, Po-sa sul lab-bro mi - o; Di vo-lut - ta dei
Sol fra' tuoi ba - ci te - ne-ri Sen-to che ho san-gue e vi - ta; Vo-glio suc-chiar - ti il

pp

cresc.

ppp

fff

ancor piano

24

neb - bria-mi, Ba-cia-mi, io tut-to o bli - o; Ba-cia-mi o ca - ra ba-cia-mi
fer - vi-do Spir - to, vo-glio suc - chiar - ti E nell'in - fi - ni - ta

fff pp

Canto di Mignon

Romanza

Antonio Ghislanzoni

Arturo Toscanini

Andante sostenuto

Ve - de - ste mai quel pa - e - se gen - til Che il

sol ri - ve - ste di tan - to splen - dor?

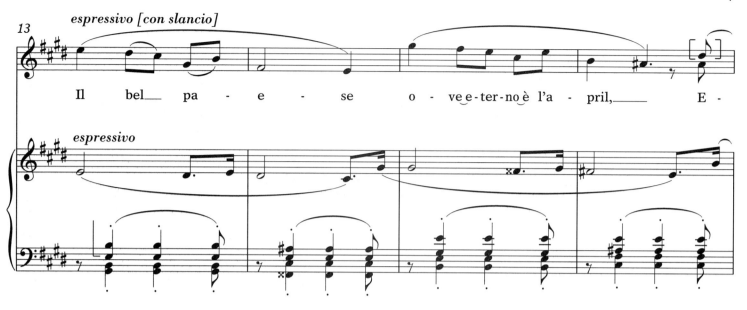

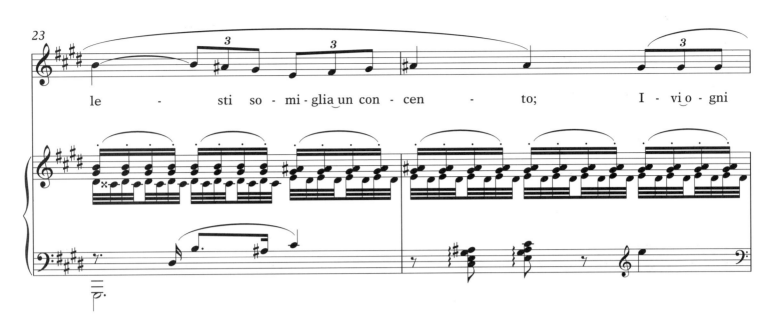

le - sti so - mi - glia un con - cen - to; I - vi o - gni

no - ta d'u - ma - na fa - ve - la, So - mi - glia un

rall.

can - to, un so - spi - ro d'a - mor.

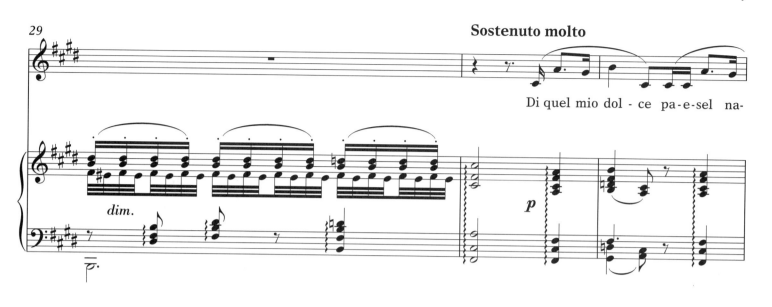

Sostenuto molto

Di quel mio dol - ce pa - e - sel na -

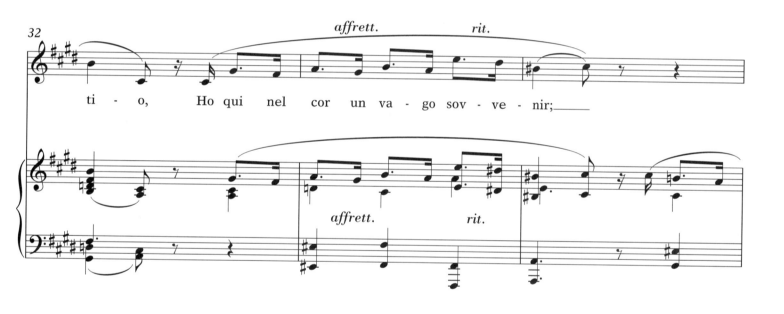

ti - o, Ho qui nel cor un va - go sov - ve - nir;

affrett. *rit.*

affrett. *rit.*

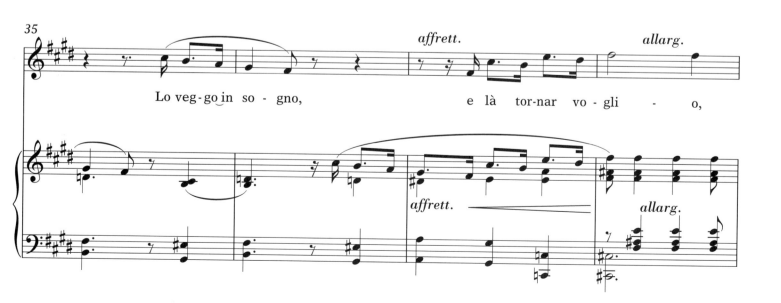

Lo veg - go in so - gno, e là tor - nar vo - gli - o,

affrett. *allarg.*

affrett. *allarg.*

10

Desolazione

Melodia

Enrico Panzacchi

Arturo Toscanini

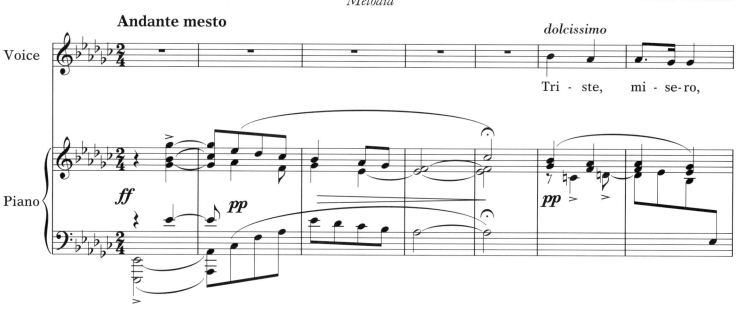

Tempo primo

La bel - lis - si - ma in - fe - del Il de -

con passione è cresc.

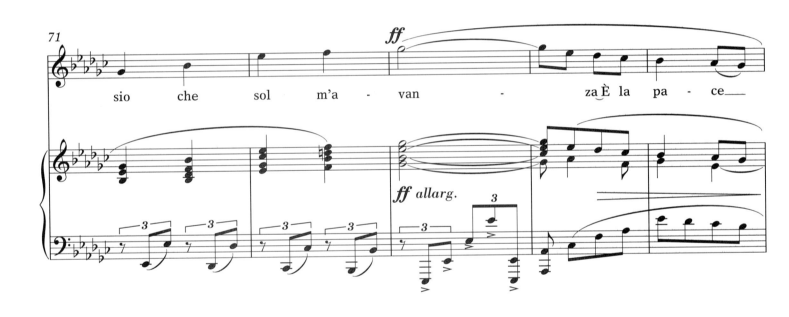

sio che sol m'a - van - za È la pa - ce

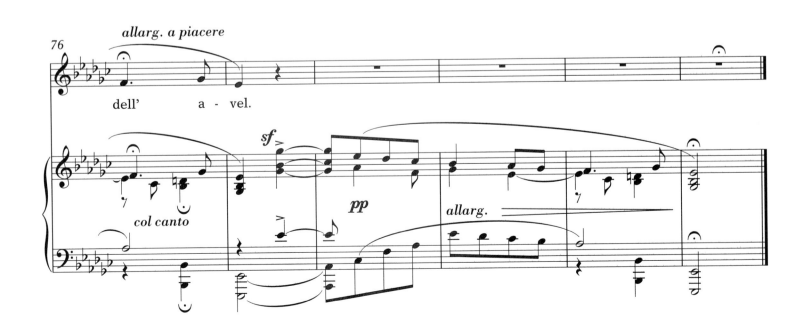

dell' a - vel.

Donna vorrei morir

Pensiero per album

Lorenzo Stecchetti

Arturo Toscanini

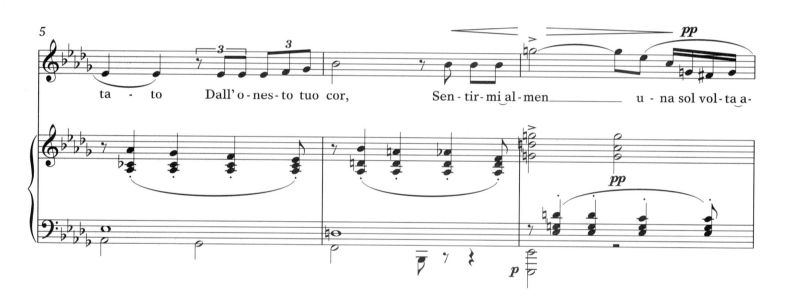

16

re - sta, quel po' che re - sta Del - la mi - a gio-ven-tù,

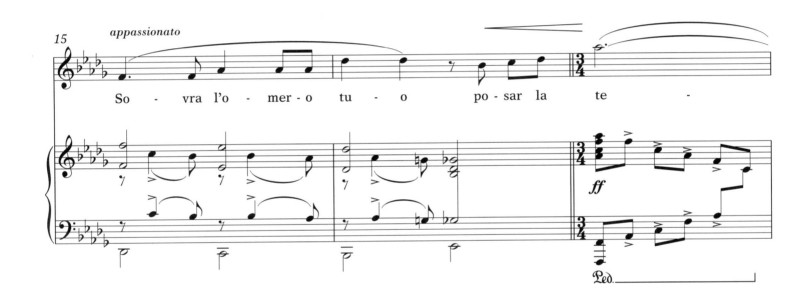

So - vra l'o - mer-o tu - o po - sar la te -

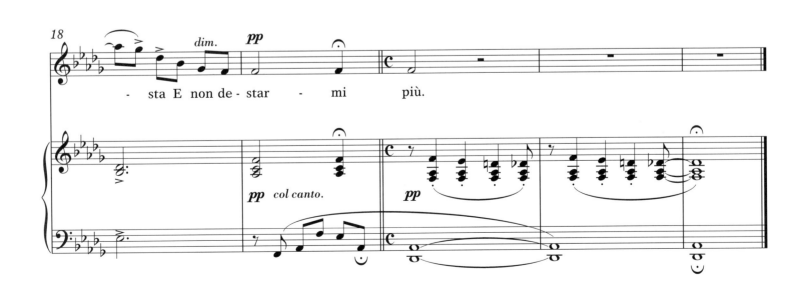

- sta E non de - star - mi più.

Fior di siepe

Lorenzo Stecchetti

Arturo Toscanini

Tu co-me l'a-mor mi - o non sei ve-du - to, Ah! Tu___ co-me l'a-mor

cresc. *affrett.* *ff* *affrett.*

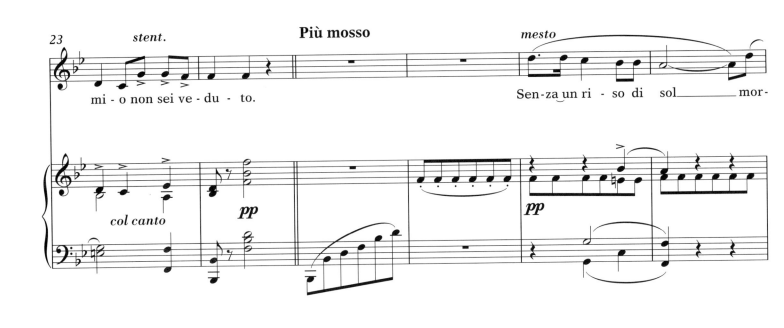

mi - o non sei ve-du - to. Sen-za un ri - so di sol_____ mor-

stent. **Più mosso** *mesto*

col canto *pp* *pp*

ra - i ser-ra - to Fra que - ste spi - ne o - ve sei cre-sciu - to:

cresc.

cresc.

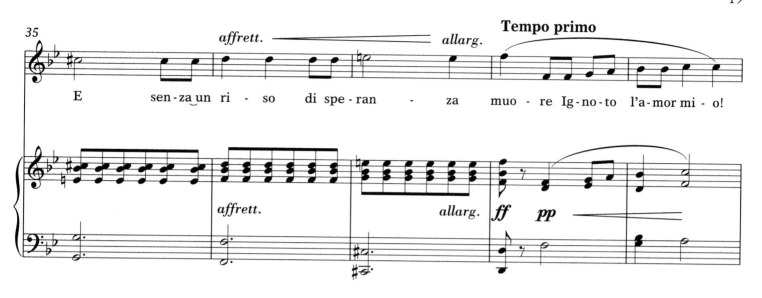

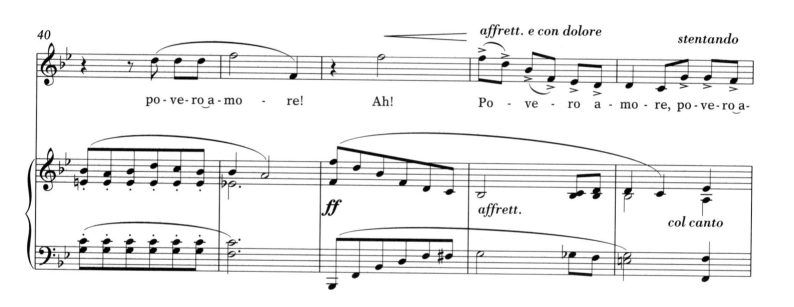

Forse una volta

Romanza

Lorenzo Stecchetti

Arturo Toscanini

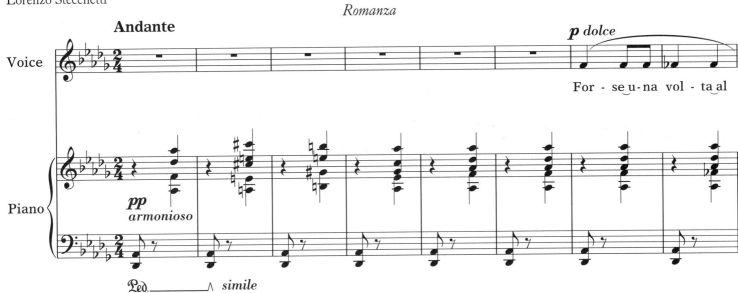

Nevrosi

Romanza

Rocco E. Pagliara

Arturo Toscanini

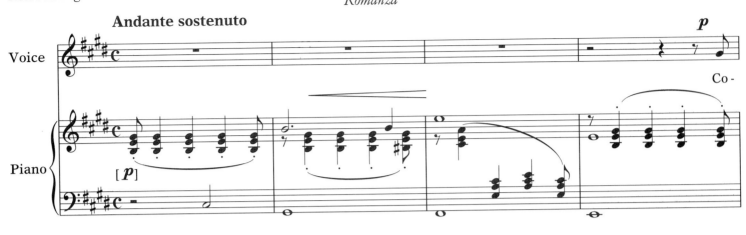

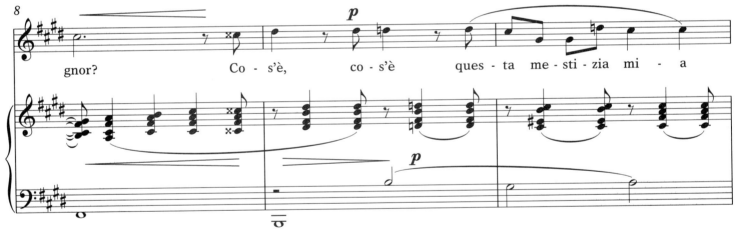

pet - to ar-den-te Nell' im-pe-to più fol - le del de - sir,_____ Vor-

rei ba-ciar-ti il cri-ne a-vi-da-men - te E poi mo-rir! E poi mo-

rir! E pian-go e ri - do, e nel tu-mul-to stra-no

pet - to_ar - den - te Nell' im-pe-to più fol - le del de - sir,___ Vor -

Largamente   **Lento**

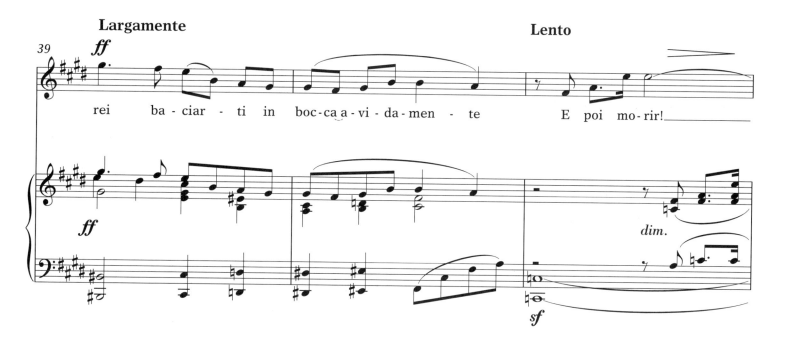

rei ba - ciar - ti in boc-ca a - vi - da-men - te E poi mo - rir!___

E poi mo - rir!___

Pagina d'album

improvvisata in scuola presente il maestro

Lorenzo Stecchetti

Arturo Toscanini

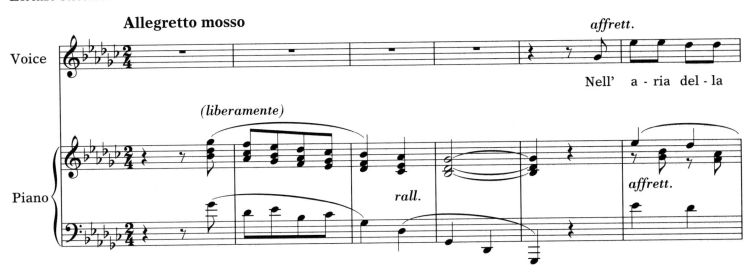

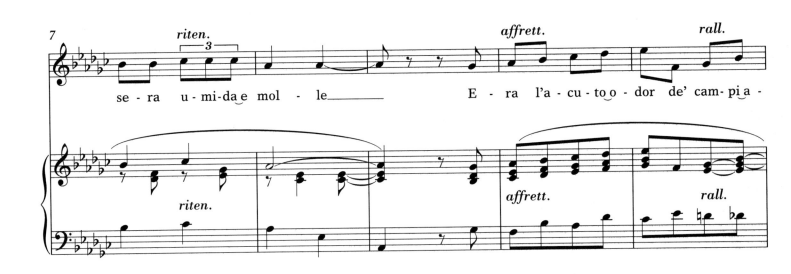

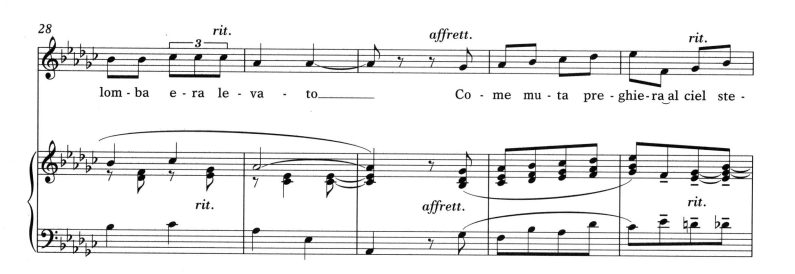

28

la - to;_____ Ed io che in-te - si quel che non di-ce - vi_____

M'in - na-mo-rai_____ di te_____ per - chè ta -

ce - vi.

Per album

Pensiero melodico

Luigi Arnaldo Vassallo

Arturo Toscanini

ri - de - re che più sor - ri - der non so Ho a - ma - to un gior - no ed

ho sof - fer - to, ho pian - to tan - to che_____ più sor - ri - der non

so che_____ più sor - ri - der non so.

Il pescatore

Ballatella

Anon.

Arturo Toscanini

u - na bion - da ver - gi - ne fu - or dall' on - da u - sci.

[poco rit.]   [poco meno mosso]

Al

che con ar - ti per - fi - de co - si____ Di - ce - a vuoi tu at -

trar a mor - te bar - ba - ra la mia gen - til tri - bù____ Ah

se sa - pe - si i gau - di che ha il pes - cio - lin quag -

giù_____ Con noi vor - res - ti scen - de - re per

non ve - nir più sù,_____ per non ve - nir più

a tempo

mp

su_____ per non ve - nir__ più su.

mp

Presentimenti

Antonio Ghislanzoni

Romanza

Arturo Toscanini

Piano

Andante

pp *dolcissimo*

dolcissimo

I - o ti chieg - go se m'a - mi, e mi ri - spon - di Io

leggiero

t'a - mo, t'a - mo as - sa - i, Io t'a - mo, t'a - mo as - sa - i.

pp

pp

I - o ti chieg - go se sem - pre m'a - me - ra - i,

pp

pp

Primo bacio

Melodia

Luigi Morandi

Arturo Toscanini

Ma non si scor-da il ba - cio dell' a - mo - re   Fin - chè la vi - ta

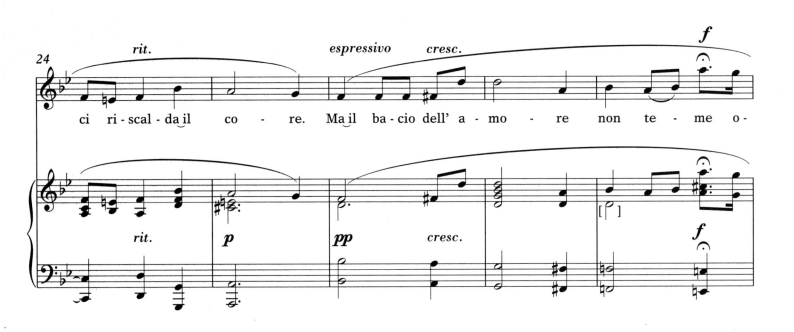

ci ri - scal - da il co - re. Ma il ba - cio dell' a - mo - re non te - me o -

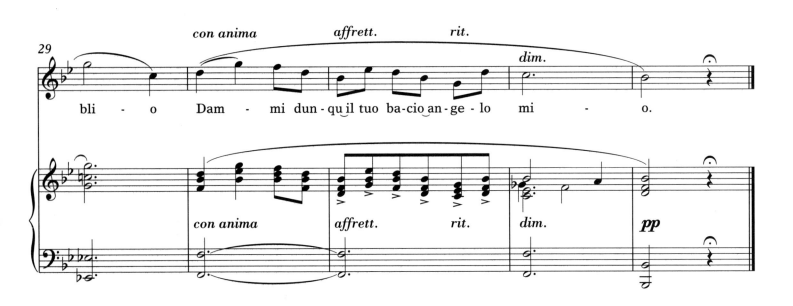

bli - o   Dam - mi dun - qu il tuo ba - cio an - ge - lo mi - o.

Quando cadran le foglie

Lorenzo Stecchetti

Romanza

Arturo Toscanini

Andante molto

Piano

Quan - do ca-dran le fo - glie e tu ver - rai A cer-

ca - re la mi - a cro - ce in cam - po-san - to

In un can-tuc - cio la ri-tro-ve-rai E mol-ti fior, e mol-ti

pel - li_____ I fio - ri na - ti dal_ mio cor, dal mi - o

Tempo I

co - re.

Son quel - li I can - ti, che pen-sai ma che non

scris - si, Le pa-ro - le d'a - mor che non ti dis -

si, che non ti dis - si, Le pa -

ro - le d'a - mor che non ti dis - si.

Son gelosa!!

Romanza

Rocco E. Pagliara

Arturo Toscanini

lo - sa, Io son ge - lo - sa di te! Son ge - lo - sa di

te! Se ti ve - do par-

tir, da___ me,___ da me lon - ta - no

Par - mi che va - da vi - a con te la

lu - ce; Co - me u-na for - za di po - ter sov - ra - no,

A te d'ap - pres - so il pen-sier mio con - du - ce. In - vi - dio i

fio - ri e l'er-ba ru - gia - do - sa, Che cal - pes-ti col piè. Ah!_____ Io

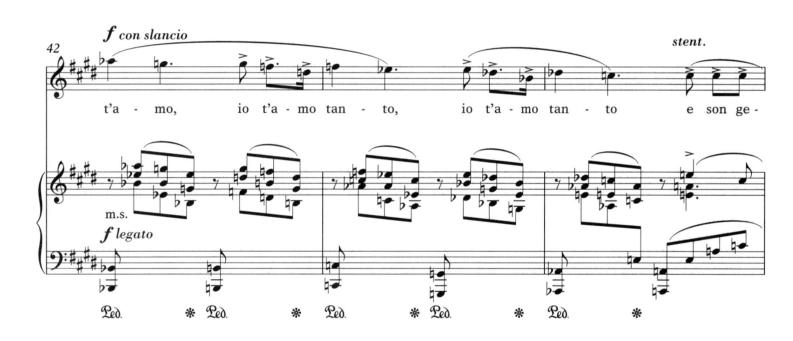

t'a - mo, io t'a-mo tan - to, io t'a-mo tan - to e son ge-

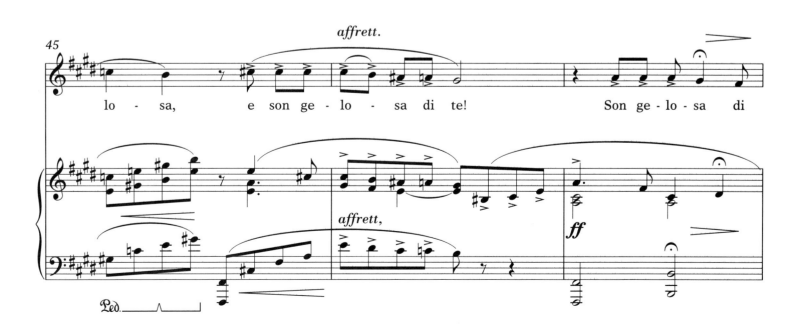

lo - sa, e son ge-lo - sa di te! Son ge-lo - sa di

48

dolcis.

te!   Non chie - der - mi per -

pp

cresc.

chè   ta - cer vo - gl'io, Ta - lor   rav - vol - ta in tor - bi - di pen - sie -

cresc.

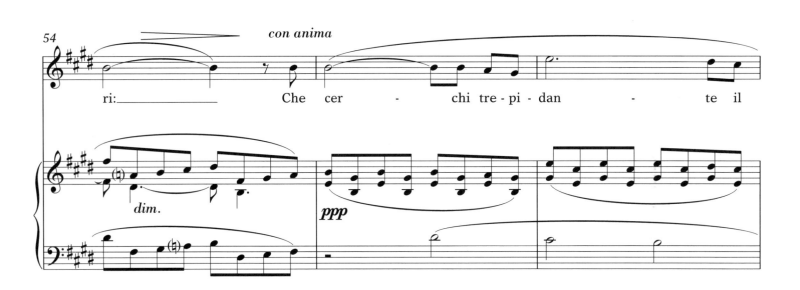

con anima

ri:_____ Che   cer - chi tre - pi - dan - te il

dim.

ppp

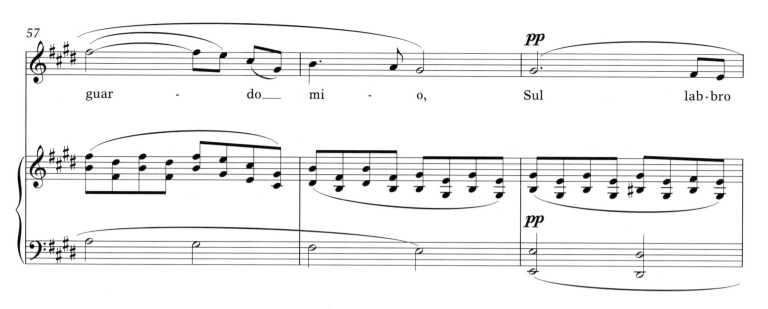

guar - do___ mi - o, Sul lab-bro

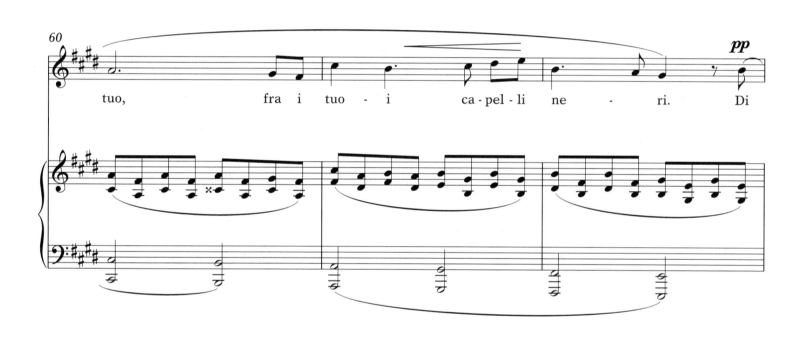

tuo, fra i tuo - i ca-pel-li ne - ri. Di

ba-ci e di ca-rez - za al-trui a - sco-sa U-na trac - cia sol v'è.___

50

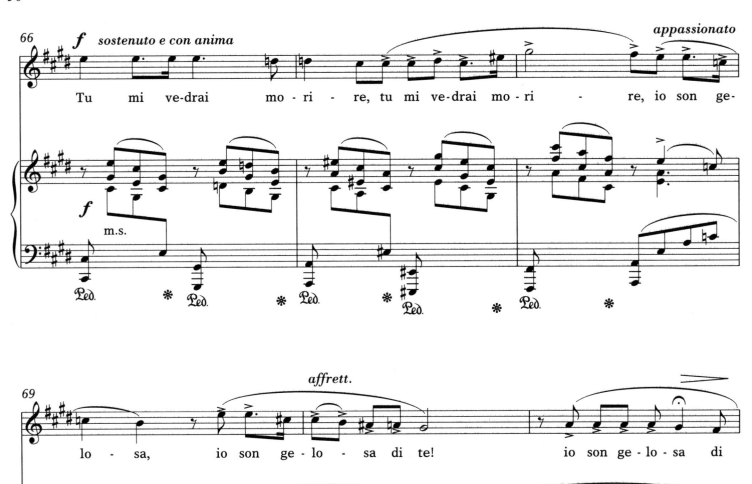

Tu mi ve-drai mo-ri - re, tu mi ve-drai mo-ri - re, io son ge-

lo - sa, io son ge-lo - sa di te! io son ge-lo - sa di

te!

Sono sola!

Romanza

Cesare Cantù

Arturo Toscanini

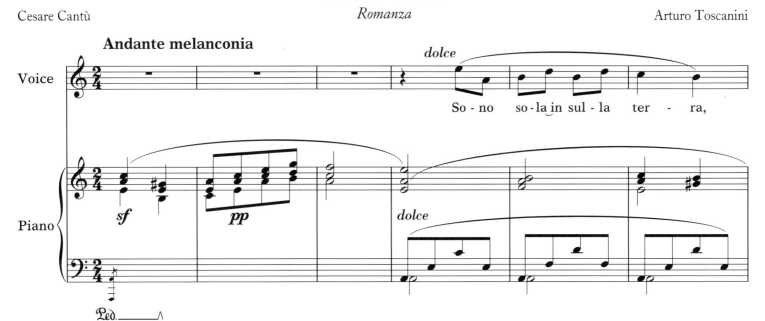

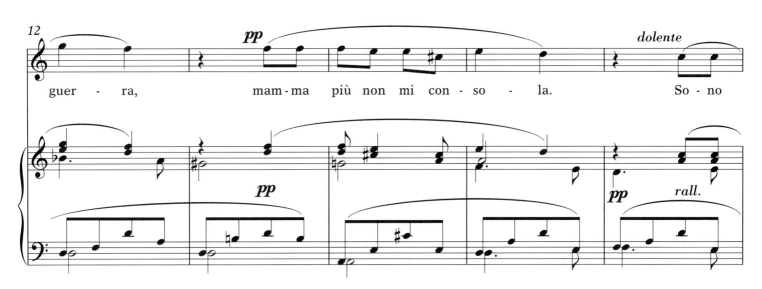

so - la, so - no so - la. Ah!

Tempo primo

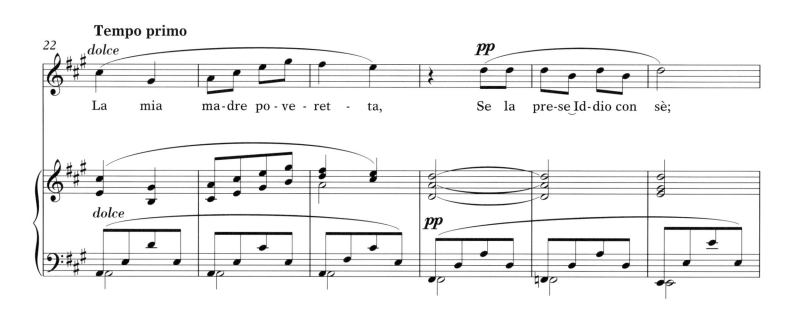

La mia ma-dre po - ve - ret - ta, Se la pre-se Id-dio con sè;

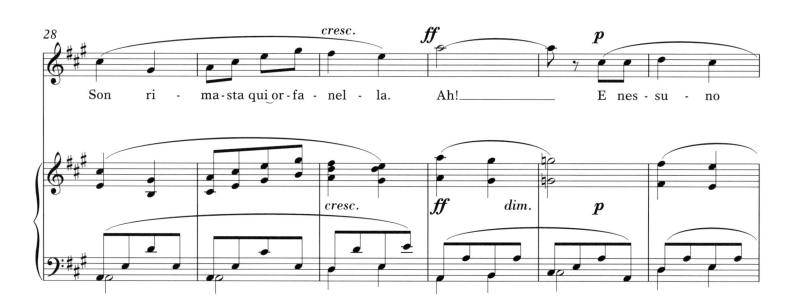

Son ri - ma-sta qui or-fa - nel - la. Ah!_____ E nes - su - no

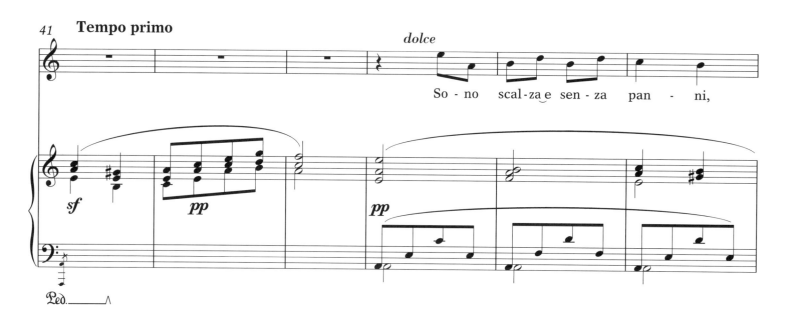

52

pp dolente

fan - ni   È tra - pun - ta la mia vi - ta.   So - no

dim.   *pp*   *pp*

57

so - la,   so - no so - la.   Ah!

rall.   *ppp*

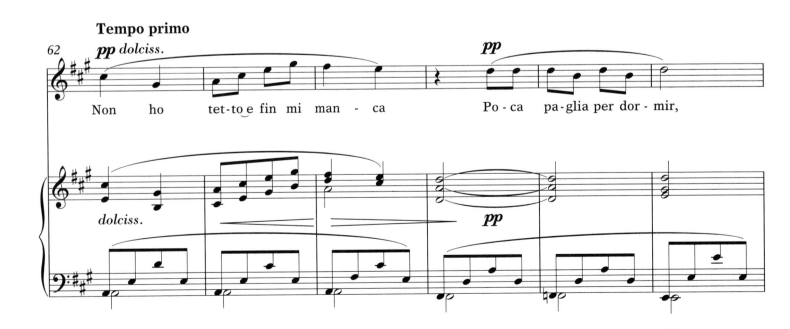

Tempo primo

62   *pp dolciss.*   *pp*

Non ho tet-to e fin mi man - ca   Po - ca pa-glia per dor - mir,

dolciss.   *pp*

So - no so - la, so - no stan - ca, Ah!_____ Me - glio fia per

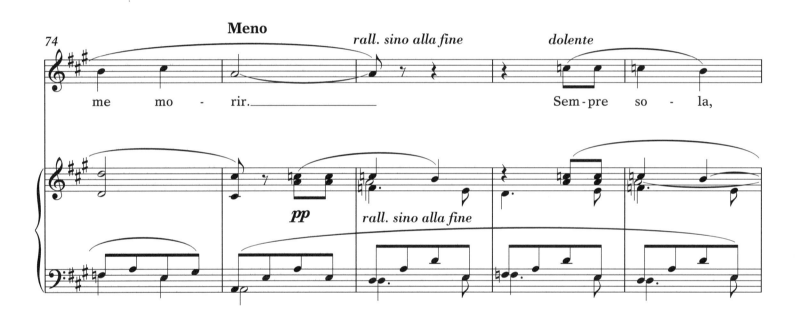

me mo - rir._____ Sem - pre so - la,

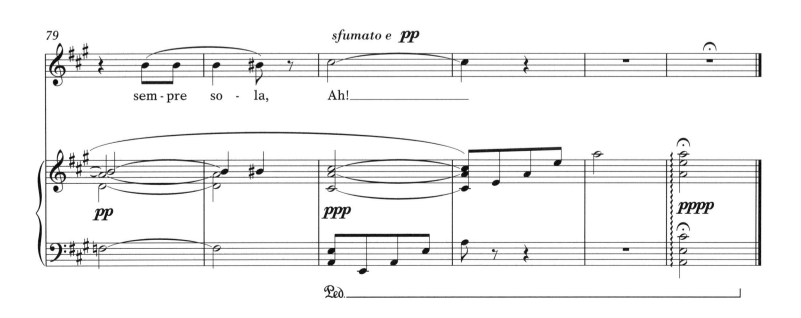

sem - pre so - la, Ah!_____

Il sorriso e l'anima di Margherita

Romanza

Angelo Rossi

Arturo Toscanini

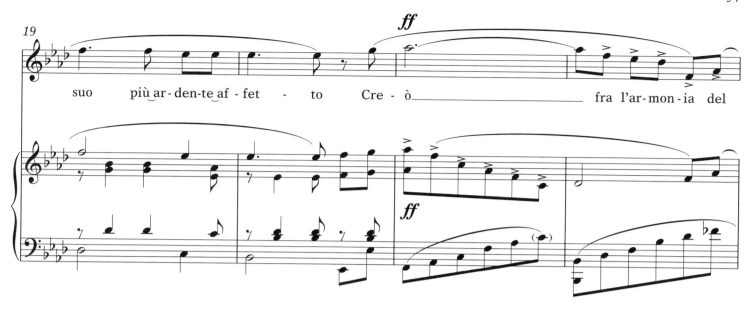

suo più ar-den-te af-fet - to Cre - ò_____ fra l'ar-mon-ia del

pa - ra - di - so.

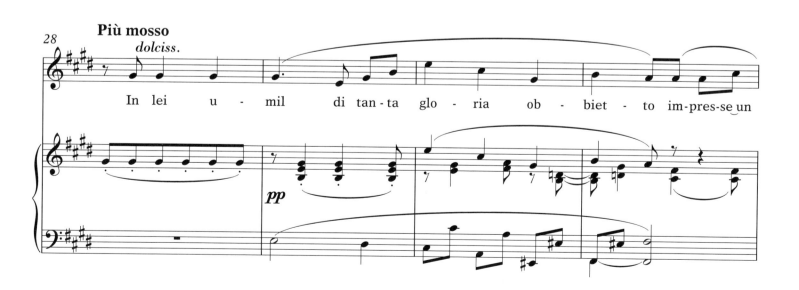

In lei u - mil di tan - ta glo - ria ob - biet - to im-pres-se un

58

Spes, ultima dea

Lorenzo Stecchetti

Arturo Toscanini

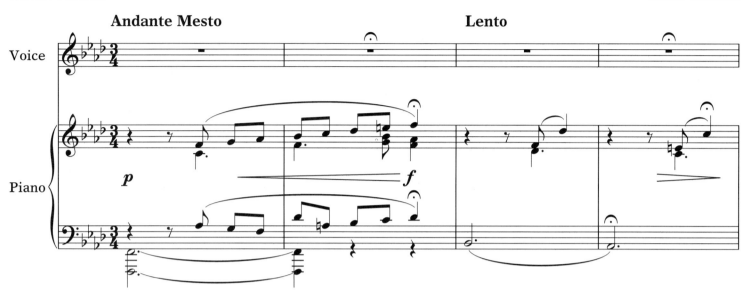

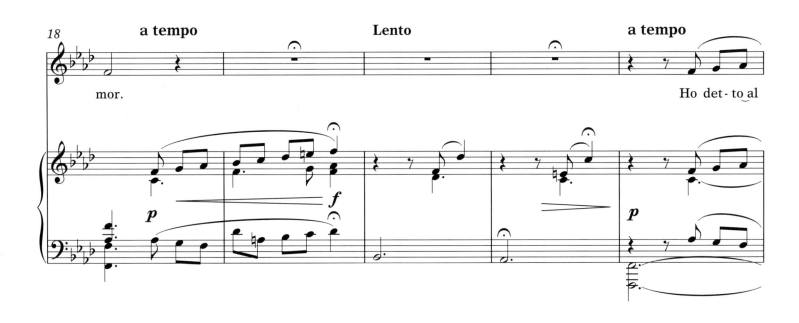

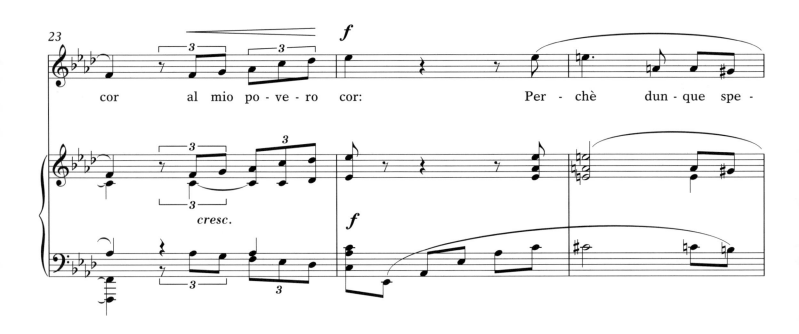

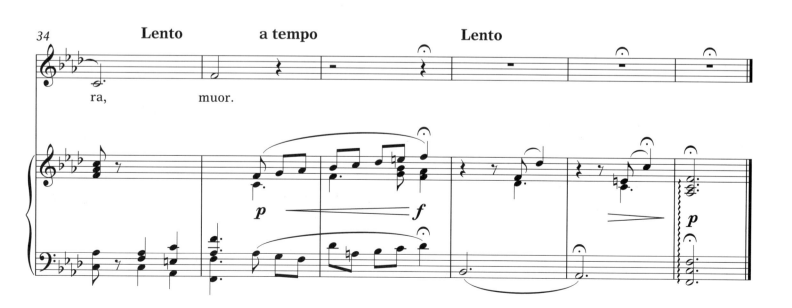

V'amo

Romanzetta

Heinrich Heine

Arturo Toscanini

vol - ta an - cor ve - der - ti io bra - mo, In - gi - noc-chiar - mi

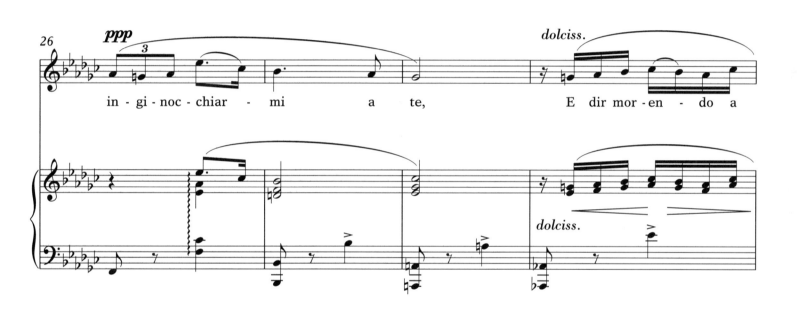

in - gi - noc - chiar - mi a te, E dir mor - en - do a

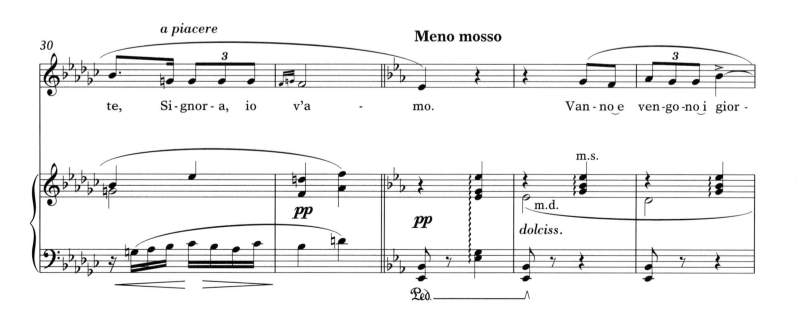

te, Si - gnor - a, io v'a - mo. Van - no e ven - go - no i gior -

Editorial Notes

Editorial additions or suggestions are shown in the score by square brackets. Obvious musical errors have been corrected without comment. Toscanini's sometimes extreme dynamic markings have been moderated and untidy phrase marks have been adjusted. Other editorial decisions are indicated in the notes below. In most cases, the New York manuscripts resolve errors found in the published editions, and these sources have usually been preferred.

Toscanini's minor variants from the texts of the original poems have been retained in the scores. Significant variants from the original poems are indicated in the editorial notes.

Ad una donna

Bars 9-10	Giuseppe Giusti poem: ...*soave tenero amplesso.*

Autunno

Bars 11-12	We have reverted to the manuscript version which is clear in intent. The typographical layout of the published score was incorrect (see also bars 21-24).
Bars 13-14	Ricordi edition: *Povero amor.*
Bars 21-24	Reverted to manuscript version (see above).

I baci

Bars 9-10	Alfio Belluso poem : *D'amor non han tal riso.*
Bars 9-10	Alfio Belluso poem : *Questo piacer mi rende.*

Canto di Mignon

Bar 39	The published version does not give the melody in octaves.
Bar 41	This bar is problematical. In the published edition and manuscripts, the vocal line and accompaniment are incompatible, creating dissonances that are not typical of the composer. In the present edition we have offered a solution by replacing B sharps with B naturals in both hands of the accompaniment, and substituting G sharp instead of A in the vocal part for the last quaver of the bar.

Donna vorrei morir

Bars 5-6	Lorenzo Stecchetti poem: Dall' onesto tuo amor
Bars 15-17	Lorenzo Stecchetti poem: Sovra l'omero tuo piegar la testa

Fior di siepe

Bar 31	Manuscript gives F sharp.
Bars 31-33	Lorenzo Stecchetti poem: *Tra queste spine dove sei cresciuto.*

Forse una volta

Bars 15-22	The piano part is incomplete. The manuscript gives only bars 15-17 of the r.h. The remainder has been reconstructed by the Editors.
Bar 28	Lorenzo Stecchetti poem: *Una lacrima...*

Nevrosi

Bars 7-8	Milan manuscript copy gives: *Questa tristezza che m'oprime il cor?*
Bar 34	The published edition extends the soprano note for an additional bar. In one of the New York manuscripts this extra bar is decisively crossed out. The other manuscript omits it altogether.

Pagina d'album

Bars 30-32	Lorenzo Stecchetti poem: *Quasi muta preghiera...*

Il pescatore

Bar 46	In the New York manuscript, a second verse is clearly indicated, but no new text is shown.

Quando cadran le foglie

Bars 18-24	Lorenzo Stecchetti poem: *E molti fior le saran nati accanto.*
Bars 25-27	Lorenzo Stecchetti poem: *Cògli allora pe' tuoi biondi capelli.*

Sono sola

Bars 22-24	Cesare Cantù poem: *La mia mamma poveretta.*
Bars 25-27	Cesare Cantù poem: *Se la presse Iddio con sè.*
Bars 68-70	Toscanini's manuscript gives *Sono stanca, sono stanca.* We have reverted to the stronger version of the original poem *Sono sola, sono stanca.*

V'amo

Bars 26/27	Misprinted as *Inginochiarmi* in published version.

Autunno

Text: Felice Carlo Cavallotti (1842-1898). Manuscript: New York Public Library (Rose Bampton Collection) headed *Autunno (Foglio d'album)*. Publisher: Milano: F. Lucca, 1888. New edition: Milano: Ricordi, 1913 Dedication (published edition): Emma Gorin. Date of composition: ca 1884.

Autumn

Dagli alberi le foglie vanno via,
Ed il mesto amor mio così sen va;
Sorride del creato all'agonia,
Ma l'aprile novel non rivedrà.

Povero amore de' verd' anni miei
Il torbido destin segui così;
Nei campi del dolor cresciuto sei,
Or compi nel dolor l'ultimo dì.

The leaves fall from the trees
And in the same way my sad love departs;
Smiles at the agony of creation,
But he will not see the new Spring.

Unhappy love of my youth
Thus you follow your dark destiny.
You have been raised in fields of pain
And now in pain you spend your last day.

I baci

Text: Alfio Belluso (1855-1904). Manuscript: Parma. Publisher: Unpublished. Dedication (manuscript): Antonio Superchi (1816-1898). Date of composition: In folio of eight songs submitted to Giusto Daci on 18 July 1885.

Kisses

Posa sul sen fra i palpiti,
Posa, o mia bella, il viso,
Non han la terra e gli esseri,
Non han d'amor tal riso;
A noi d'intorno olezzano
Serti di gemme e fior

Posa il tuo labbro roseo,
Posa sul labbro mio;
Di voluttade inebbriami,
Baciami, io tutto oblio;
Forte ti stringo, e rompermi
Sento d'ebbrezza il cor.

Taci, chè quell' armonica
Favella più m'accende;
Muto, tremante e languido
Questo pensier mi rende;
Baciami, o cara, e lasciami
Di voluttà morir.

Sol fra' tuoi baci teneri
Sento che ho sangue e vita;
Voglio succhiarti il fervido
Spirto, e nell'infinita
Soavità confondermi
Sì, de' tuoi dolci sospir.

Rest on my beating heart,
Rest, o my beautiful, your face.
Earth has no creature more beautiful,
Love has no such splendor;
To us, surrounded with fragrance
Garlanded with buds and flowers.

Rest your red lips,
Rest them on mine;
Intoxicated by the pleasure,
Kiss me, all is oblivion.
I clasp you tightly, and I
Feel my heart burst with joy.

Be quiet, for those harmonious
Words inflame me more;
Speechless, trembling and languid
This thought makes me;
Kiss me my darling, and let me
Die from sensual pleasure.

Only amidst your tender kisses
Do I feel I have blood and life;
I want to draw from you the ardent
Spirit, and with the infinite
Gentleness of your sweet sighs,
Yes, become as one.

Canto di Mignon

Text: Antonio Ghislanzoni (1824-1893). Manuscript: New York Public Library (Rose Bampton Collection). Publisher: Torino: Giudici & Strada, 1888. Dedication (published edition): Emma Gorin. Date of composition: Manuscript dated 1884.

Mignon's song

Vedeste mai quel paese gentil
Che il sol riveste di tanto splendor?
Il bel paese ove eterno è l'april,
Eterno il riso degli astri e dei fior?

Ivi ogni murmure d'acqua o di vento,
D'arpe celesti somiglia un concento;
Ivi ogni nota d'umana favella,
Somiglia un canto, un sospiro d'amor.

Di quel mio dolce paesel natio,
Ho qui nel cor un vago sovvenir;
Lo veggo in sogno, e la tornar vogl'io,
Là voglio amar e piangere, e morir.

Have you ever seen that lovely land
That the sun clothes in such splendor?
The beautiful land where spring lasts forever.
Where the smile of the stars and flowers is everlasting.

There, any murmur of water or wind
Sounds like a concert of heavenly harps.
There, every note of human voice
Sounds like a song, a sigh of love.

Of that sweet homeland
I have in my heart a faint memory
I see it in my dreams, and I long to return there.
There I want to love, to weep and to die.

Desolazione

Text: Enrico Panzacchi (1840-1904). Manuscript: Parma. Publisher: Torino: Giudici & Strada, ca 1888.
Dedication (manuscript): Antonio Superchi. Dedication (published edition): Gemma Ferruggia
Date of composition: In folio of eight songs submitted to Giusto Daci on 18 July 1885.

Triste, misero, obliato,
Vola intorno il mio sospir;
Poche gioie ha il mio passato,
Senza riso è l'avvenir.

Dove andò la sorridente
Primavera de'miei dì?
Come foglia nel torrente,
Dal mio animo fuggì.

L'universo agli occhi miei
Solitudine si fè,
Più l'ambrosia degli Dei
Io non chiedo, o vita, a te.

Io non credo alla speranza
La bellissima infidel.
Il desio che sol m'avanza
È la pace dell'avel.

Desolation

Sad, unhappy, forgotten,
My sigh flies in the air;
Few past joys are left to me,
The future is without laughter.

Where has gone the smiling
Spring of my life?
Like a leaf in the torrent
From my soul it fled.

The universe, to my eyes,
Became solitude.
O life, no longer will I seek
The ambrosia of the Gods from you.

I do not believe in hope
The unfaithful beauty.
My only remaining desire
Is the peace of the grave.

Donna vorrei morir

Text: Lorenzo Stecchetti, pseud. of Olindo Guerrini (1845-1916). Manuscript: Parma. Dedication: Armida Barone, Genoa, April 4 [18]90.
Publisher: Unpublished. Date of composition: ca 1889

Donna vorrei morir, ma confortato
Dall'onesto tuo amor,
Sentirmi almeno una sol volta amato
Senza averne rossor.

Vorrei poterti dar quel po' che resta
Della mia gioventù,
Sovra l'omero tuo piegar la testa
E non destarmi più.

Woman, I should like to die

Woman, I should like to die, but comforted
By the honesty of your love;
To feel loved at least once
Without feeling shame.

I should like to give you what remains
Of my youth;
Rest my head on your shoulder
And never wake again.

Fior di siepe

Text: Lorenzo Stecchetti, pseud. of Olindo Guerrini (1845-1916). Manuscript: Biblioteca Palatina – Sezione musicale, Parma. Publisher:
Unpublished. Dedication (manuscript): Antonio Superchi (1816-1898). Date: In folio of eight songs submitted to Giusto Daci on 18 July 1885.

O fiorellin di siepe, all'ombra nato,
Povero fiorellin non conosciuto,
Tu come l'amor mio sei disgraziato,
Tu come l'amor mio non sei veduto.
Senza un riso di sol morrai serrato
Fra queste spine ove sei cresciuto;
E senza un riso di speranza muore
Ignoto l'amor mio... Povero amore!

Hedge-flower

Oh gentle hedge-flower born in the shade,
Poor little unknown flower,
Like my love, you are wretched.
Like my love you are unseen.
Without a smile from the sun you will close and die
Among these thorns where you were born.
And with no smile of hope dies
My love, unknown. Ah, poor love!

Forse una volta / Perhaps one day

Text: Lorenzo Stecchetti, pseud. of Olindo Guerrini (1845-1916). Manuscript (non-autograph): Conservatorio di Milano. Publisher: Unpublished. Date of composition: ca 1885.

Forse una volta al tuo balcon seduta	Perhaps one day sitting at your balcony
Della tremule stella ai bianchi rai	In the white eyes of the trembling stars
Lontan lontano per la notte udrai	You will hear a cry in the night from far away
Un grido che si spegne e ti saluta:	A cry that dies away and greets you.
Qui tra i fiori dove prima t'ho veduta	Here, among the flowers where first I saw you,
Una lagrima un dì ritroverai	One day you will find a tear,
Ma ti parrà rugiada e coglierai	But it will appear as dew and you will pick
Pè' tuoi capelli il fior dov'è caduta.	For your hair, the flower on which the tear fell.

Nevrosi / Neurosis

Text: Rocco E. Pagliara (1857-1914). Manuscripts: Conservatorio di Milano (1) and New York Public Library (Rose Bampton Collection) (2). Publisher: Milano: F. Lucca, ca.1888. Dedication (published edition): Emma Gorin. Dedication (Milan manuscript): Virginia Ferni-Germano (1849-1934). Dedication (New York manuscript coupled with *Primo bacio*): Nadina Boulicioff (1858-1921). Date of composition: ca.1885.

Cos' è, cos' è questa melanconia	What, ah what, is this melancholy
Che mi tormenta e che m'opprime ognor?	That always tortures and oppresses me?
Cos' è, cos' è questa mestizia mia	What, ah what is this sadness,
Questa nube di pianto e di dolor?	This cloud of weeping and grief?
Ahi, stringerti vorrei sul petto ardente	Ah, I long to clasp you to my ardent breast
Nell' impeto più folle del desir	In the most passionate gesture of desire.
Vorrei baciarti il crine avidamente	I long to kiss your hair avidly
E poi morir!	And then to die!
E piango e rido, e nel tumulto strano	I cry and I smile, and in this strange tumult
Raggio di pace non risplende a me;	No ray of peace shines on me.
Come sospinta da poter arcano	As if moved by secret power
Fugge l'anima mia cercando te.	My soul runs away in search of you.
Ahi, stringerti vorrei sul petto ardente	Ah I wish to clasp you to my ardent breast
Nell' impeto più folle del desir,	In the most passionate gesture of desire.
Vorrei baciarti in bocca avidamente	I am eager to kiss your lips
E poi morir!	And then to die!

Pagina d'album / Album leaf

Text: Lorenzo Stecchetti, pseud. of Olindo Guerrini (1845-1916). Published in some anthologies as *Ti amai perchè tacevi*. Manuscript: New York Public Library (Rose Bampton Collection). Publisher: Unpublished. Date of composition: Manuscript dated 1882-83.

Nell'aria della sera umida e molle	In the humid, soft evening air
Era l'acuto odor de' campi arati	Was the strong smell of ploughed fields
E noi salimmo insiem su questo colle	And we climbed this hill together
Mentre il grillo stridea laggiù nei prati.	While the crickets chirped in the meadows below.
L'occhio tuo di colomba era levato	Your dove-like eyes were raised
Come muta preghiera al ciel stellato;	As in silent prayer to the starry sky;
Ed io che intesi quel che non dicevi	And I, who understood your unspoken thoughts,
M'innamorai di te perchè tacevi.	Fell in love with you, because you were silent.

Per album / For the album

Text: Luigi Arnaldo Vassallo (1852-1906). Manuscripts: Parma and New York Public Library (Rose Bampton Collection). Publisher: Unpublished. Dedication (Parma manuscript): Ester Barone, Genoa, April 2 [18]90. Date of composition: ca1889.

Se tu mi chiedi perché più non canto	If you ask me why I sing no more
Diletto angelo mio te lo dirò;	My darling angel, I will tell you;
Ho amato un giorno ed ho sofferto, ho pianto	Once I loved and suffered and wept
Tanto che più che sorridere non so.	So much that I no longer know how to smile.

Il pescatore   ## The fisherman

Text: Unidentified. Manuscripts: Parma and New York Public Library (Rose Bampton Collection).
Publisher: Unpublished. Dedication (Parma manuscript): Antonio Superchi (1816-1898).
Date: New York Public Library manuscript dated 1882-1883. In folio of eight songs submitted to Giusto Daci on 18 July 1885.

D'un vago fiume al margine s'assise un pescator Guardando all'esca turgida ridente a baldo in cor. Ma in quella un fiero vortice il flutto disunì Ed una bionda vergine fuor dall'onda uscì.	On the bank of a fair river sat an angler, Looking at the succulent bait with confident heart. But suddenly a strong whirlpool stirred the waters, And a blond maiden arose from the waves.
A che con arti perfide così dicea: Vuoi tu attrar a morte barbara la mia gentil tribù Ah se sapessi i gaudi che ha il pesciolin quaggiù Con noi vorresti scendere per non venir più su.	Then with treachorous art she said: You want to draw to cruel death my gentle kind. Ah, if only you knew the joy the little fish has down here, You would want to come down with us, and never return.

Presentimenti   ## Forbodings

Text: Antonio Ghislanzoni (1824-1893). Manuscript: Location unknown. Publisher: Unpublished. Dedication: Brigida Varron.
Date of composition: ca 1885.

Io ti chieggo se m'ami, e mi rispondi Io t'amo, t'amo assai. Io ti chieggo se sempre m'amerai Tu taci e il viso ascondi.	I ask if you love me and you reply I love very much. I ask if you will always love me You are silent and hide your face.
De' tuoi silenzi o dolce mia fanciulla Il triste arcan io scerno Tu sai che m'ami e sai che al par del nulla Avvi quaggiù d'eterno.	From your silence my sweet lady I understand the sad reason You know you love me and you know that Nothing in this world can last forever.

Primo bacio   ## First kiss

Text: Luigi Morandi (1844-1922). Manuscripts: Conservatorio di Milano and New York Public Library (Rose Bampton Collection).
Publisher: Unpublished. Dedication (New York manuscript, coupled with *Nevrosi*): Nadina Boulicioff (1858-1921).
Date of composition: Milan manuscript dated 13 August 1889.

Si scorda la preghiera della culla Vanno insieme in oblio letizie e guai Si scorda Iddio né ci spaventa il nulla Ma il primo bacio non si scorda mai	One forgets the prayers said in the cradle, Delights and worries are forgotten together. One forgets God, nor does oblivion frighten us. But one never forgets the first kiss.
Mai non si scorda il bacio dell'amore Finchè la vita ci riscalda il core. Ma il bacio dell'amor non teme oblio Dammi dunque il tuo bacio angelo mio.	One never forgets the kiss of love As long as life warms our heart. But the kiss of love fears not oblivion, So give me your kiss, my angel.

Quando cadran le foglie   ## When the leaves fall

Text: Lorenzo Stecchetti, pseud. of Olindo Guerrini (1845-1916). Manuscript: New York Public Library (Rose Bampton Collection).
Publisher: Unpublished. Date of composition: ca 1885.

Quando cadran le foglie e tu verrai A cercare la mia croce in camposanto, In un cantuccio la ritroverai E molti fiori saranno nati accanto.	When the leaves fall and you come To seek my cross in the cemetery, You will find it in a little corner With many flowers in bloom around.
Cogli allor tu pe' tuoi biondi capelli I fiori nati dal mio core. Son quelli	Gather then for your blond hair The flowers born from my heart. They are
I canti che pensai ma che non scrissi, Le parole d'amor che non ti dissi.	The songs I thought but did not write, The words of love I did not say to you.

Son gelosa!   ## I am gealous!

Text: Rocco E. Pagliara (1857-1914). Manuscripts: Parma and New York (Rose Bampton Collection). The New York manuscript is an incomplete version transposed up a semitone (F major). Dedication (manuscript): Antonio Superchi (1816-1898). Dedication (published edition): Adele Borghi. Publisher: Torino: Giudici & Strada, c1888. Date of composition: In folio of eight songs submitted to Giusto Daci on 18 July 1885.

Mi trema il cor, se il guardo tuo soltanto
Indifferente un'altra affisa in volto;
D'improvviso mi vien sul ciglio il pianto,
Se volgere ad un'altra il dir t'ascolto.
Il guardo tuo, la voce armonioso
Voglio solo per me.
Io t'amo, io t'amo tanto e son gelosa,
Son gelosa di te!

My heart trembles if you simply look
At the face of another woman;
Suddenly tears come to my eyes.
If I hear you simply speak to another woman
Your gaze, your harmonious voice
I want only for myself.
I love you, I love you so much and I am jealous
I am jealous of you.

Se ti vedo partir, da me lontano
Parmi che vada via con te la luce.
Come una forza di poter sovrano
A te d'appresso il pensier mio conduce.
Invidio i fior e l'erba rugiadosa,
Che calpesti col piè .
Io t'amo, io t'amo tanto e son gelosa,
Son gelosa di te!

If I see you go far from me
I feel the light goes away with you.
As if pulled by sovereign power
My thoughts go with you.
I envy the flowers and the dewy grass
You trample underfoot.
I love you, I love you so much and I am jealous
I am jealous of you.

Non chiedermi perchè tacer vogl'io,
Talor ravvolta in torbidi pensieri:
Che cerchi trepidante il guardo mio,
Sul labbro tuo, fra i tuoi capelli neri.
Di baci e di carezze altrui ascosa
Una traccia sol v'è.
Tu mi vedrai morire, io son gelosa,
Son gelosa di te!

Do not ask why I wish to be silent
Sometimes dark thoughts absorb me
As my anxious gaze searches
On your lips and among your dark hair
For just a trace of kisses and caresses
From someone else.
You will see me die, I am jealous
I am jealous of you.

Sono sola!   ## I am alone!

Text: Cesare Cantù (1804-1895). Manuscripts: Parma and New York Public Library (Rose Bampton Collection). Dedication (Parma manuscript): Antonio Superchi (1816-1898). Dedication (New York manuscript): *A mio Maestro Primo Giusto. In segno di stima e riconoscenza.* Publisher: Unpublished. Date of composition: In folio of eight songs submitted to Giusto Daci on 18 July 1885.

Sono sola in sulla terra,
Nel villaggio sono sola
Il mio babbo è morto in guerra,
Mamma più non mi consola.
Sono sola. Ah!

I am alone on this earth.
In the village I am alone.
My father died in war.
My mother can no longer comfort me
I am alone. Ah.

La mia madre poveretta
Se la prese Iddio con sè;
Son rimasta qui orfanella. Ah!
E nessuno pensa a me.
Sempre sola. Ah!

God has taken
My poor mother.
I am left here as an orphan.
Ah! No-one cares for me.
Always alone. Ah!

Sono scalza e senza panni
Senza pane e senza aita,
Ah, Signor di quanti affanni
È trapunta la mia vita.
Sono sola. Ah!

I'm barefoot and without clothes,
Without bread and without help.
Ah God, so many troubles
Have occurred in my life.
I am alone. Ah!

Non ho tetto e fin mi manca
Poca paglia per dormir
Sono sola, sono stanca,
Meglio fia per me morir.
Sempre sola. Ah!

I have no roof and even lack
Straw to sleep on.
I am alone, I am weary
Ah! It would be better to die.
Always alone. Ah!

Il sorriso e l'anima di Margherita*

Text: Angelo Rossi. Manuscripts: Parma and New York Public Library (Rose Bampton Collection). The New York manuscript is titled *L'anima ed il sorriso di Margherita*. Dedication (Parma manuscript): Antonio Superchi (1816-1898). Publisher: Unpublished. Date of composition: In folio of eight songs submitted to Giusto Daci on 18 July 1885.

Il sorriso e l'anima di Margherita*
L'alma che splende nel regale aspetto
E fa celeste il guardo e il dolce riso
Il Trino Amor nel suo più ardente affetto
Creò fra l'armonia del paradiso.

In lei umil di tanta gloria obbietto
Impresse un raggio d'immortal sorriso
Sarai per cuor - le disse - e per ingegno
Delizia e orgoglio dell'Ausonio Regno.

*Queen Margherita of Savoy

The smile and soul of Margherita*

The smile and soul of Margherita*
The soul that gleams forth from the regal visage
And makes celestial the eyes and sweet the smile,
Was created by God's profound love
In the harmony of paradise.

In her, who is the humble object of so much glory,
God sealed a ray of an immortal smile.
Through reason and through your heart, He told her,
You will be the delight and the pride of the Italian Kingdom.

Spes, ultima dea*

Text: Lorenzo Stecchetti, pseud. of Olindo Guerrini (1845-1916). Manuscripts: Parma and New York Public Library (Rose Bampton Collection). Dedication (Parma manuscript): Antonio Superchi (1816-1898). The New York manuscript has the name of violinist Enrico Pollo on the cover. Publisher: Unpublished. Date of composition: In folio of eight songs submitted to Giusto Daci on 18 July 1885.

Ho detto al cor, al mio povero cor:
– Perchè questo sconforto questo languor? –
Ed egli m'ha risposto: – È morto amor! –

Ho detto al cor, al mio povero cor:
– Perchè dunque sperar se amor è morto? –
Ed egli m'ha risposto: – Chi non spera, muor.

*In Roman mythology, Spes was the goddess of hope.

Spes, the last goddess*

I said to my heart, to my poor heart,
– Why this dejection, this languor? –
And it answered: – Love is dead–.

I said to my heart, to my poor heart,
– Why hope then, if love is dead? –
And it answered, – He who hopes not, dies.

V'amo

Text: Heinrich Heine (1797-1856). Manuscript: New York Public Library (Rose Bampton Collection). Dedication: Guido Rocchi. Published: Torino: Guidici & Strada, 1889. Date of composition: ca 1885.

Vanno e vengono i giorni, i mesi, gli anni;
Pur mai l'amor in me
Non si strugge, nutrito sol d'affanni!

Sol una volta ancor vederti io bramo,
Inginocchiarmi a te,
E dir morendo a te: Signora, io v'amo.

I love you

Days, months and years come and go;
Yet the love I feel
Is never consumed, nourished only by distress.

I long to see you just once again,
To kneel before you,
Then to die while saying to you: Lady I love you.

Translations by Lia Contursi, Roger Flury, Marian Minson, Federica Riva and Marco Sonzogni

Acknowledgements

Without the support and encouragement of the following individuals this publication would not have been possible:
Raffaella Nardella and Federica Riva (Conservatorio di Musica 'Arrigo Boito', Parma); Marco Sonzogni (Victoria University of Wellington); Massimo Carnelos (Ambasciata d'Italia, Wellington); Adrienne Baron, Tim Dodd, Des Wilson, David McCaw and Kate Mead (Radio New Zealand Concert); Bob Kosovsky (Music Division, The New York Public Library for the Performing Arts); Massimo Gentili-Tedeschi (Biblioteca Nazionale Braidense, Milan); Agostina Zecca Laterza (Conservatorio di Milano 'Giuseppe Verdi'); Erik Bruchez (Switzerland); Lia Contursi (University of Canterbury, Christchurch); Konrad Dryden (Bamberg); Richard Hardie, Ben Morrison and Vyvan Yendoll (Wellington); Pavel Kordik (Prague); Harvey Sachs (Italy); Allan Steckler (New York), and my colleagues Christopher Anderson, Peter Downes, Keith McEwing and Marion Minson (Alexander Turnbull Library, National Library of New Zealand).

In 2007, the orchestra of the School of Music, Victoria University (now the New Zealand School of Music) sight-read four orchestral works by Toscanini in an open rehearsal, conducted by David Vine. The same year, to mark the 50th anniversary of Arturo Toscanini's death, Radio New Zealand Concert recorded a talk by Roger Flury on the songs of Arturo Toscanini. This featured sixteen songs, performed by Patricia Wright (soprano), Patrick Power (tenor) and David Vine (piano). The program was first broadcast on 29 November 2007 and repeated on 15 October 2009.

In 2008 a second program featured Des Wilson's interview with Roger Flury on the non-vocal music of Toscanini. The chamber music for strings was performed by Kristina Zelinska (solo violin), Cindy Yan and Miyo Yoon (violins), Vyvyan Yendoll (viola), and Paul Mitchell (cello). The solo piano works were performed by David Vine and the program was first broadcast on 29 October 2009.

Thanks are therefore due to all the artists who participated so willingly in these events to honor Toscanini, and to the organizations who offered their venues and technical expertise; Radio New Zealand Concert, The National Library of New Zealand, Victoria University of Wellington, The New Zealand School of Music and The University of Auckland.

Roger Flury
David Vine

Wellingon, New Zealand
December 2009